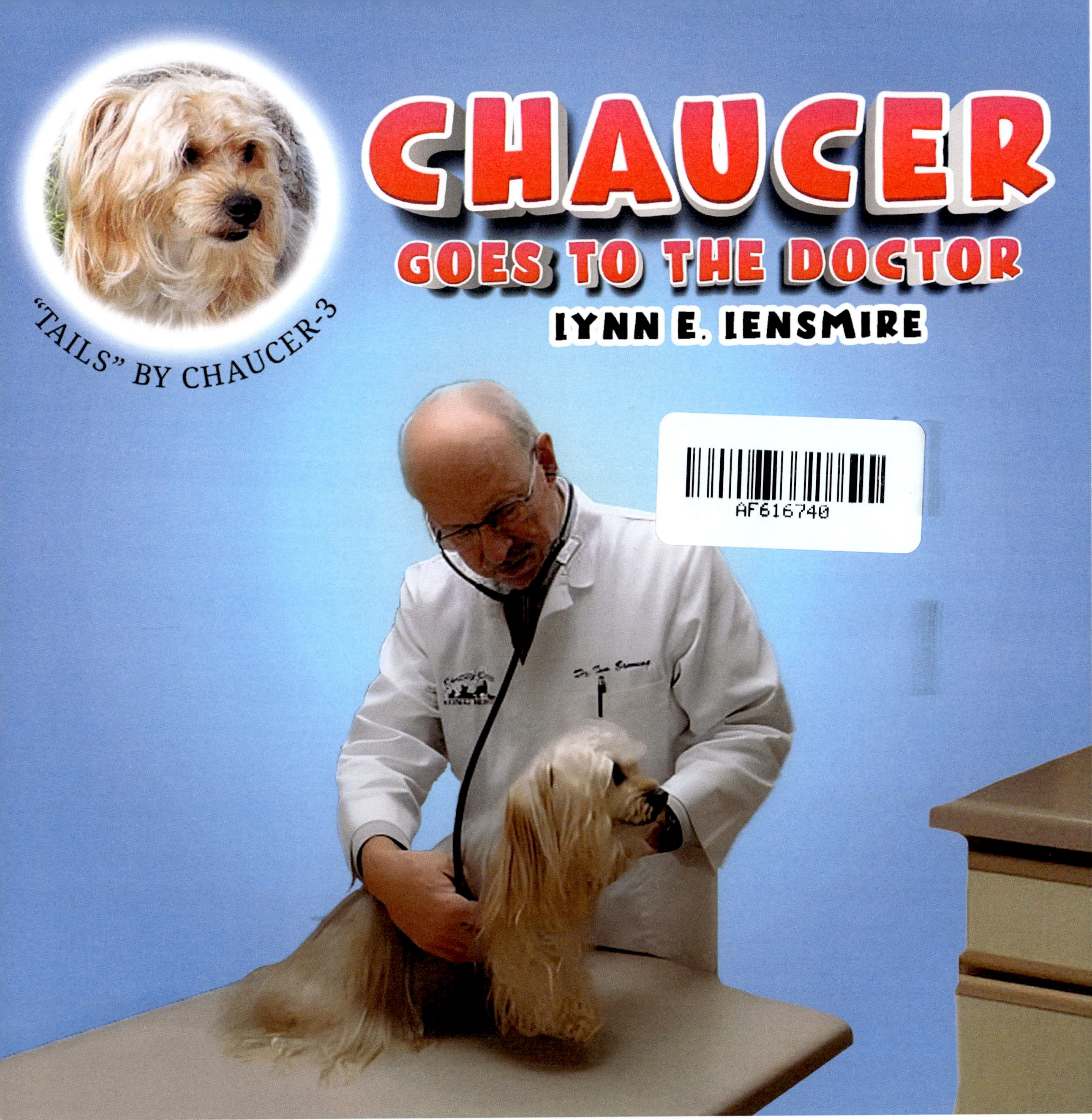
CHAUCER
GOES TO THE DOCTOR
LYNN E. LENSMIRE
"TAILS" BY CHAUCER-3
AF616740

To John, Sarah, Amanda, Kyle, Krystal, Megan, Andrew, Noa, Grace, Aliya, Isabelle, Jacob, and Roman; thank you for making this world a more beautiful place. Hugs

Published in the United States of America

ISBN 978-1-963379-52-5 (SC)
ISBN 978-1-963379-50-1 (HC)
ISBN 978-1-963379-51-8 (Ebook)

Lynn Lensmire Books
222 West 6th Street
Suite 400, San Pedro, CA, 90731
lynnandjohnl@frontier.com

Order Information and Rights Permission:

Quantity sales. Special discounts might be available on quantity purchases by corporations, associations, and others. For details, contact the publisher at the address above.

For Book Rights Adaptation and other Rights Permission.
Call us at toll-free 1-888-945-8513 or send us an email at
admin@stellarliterary.com

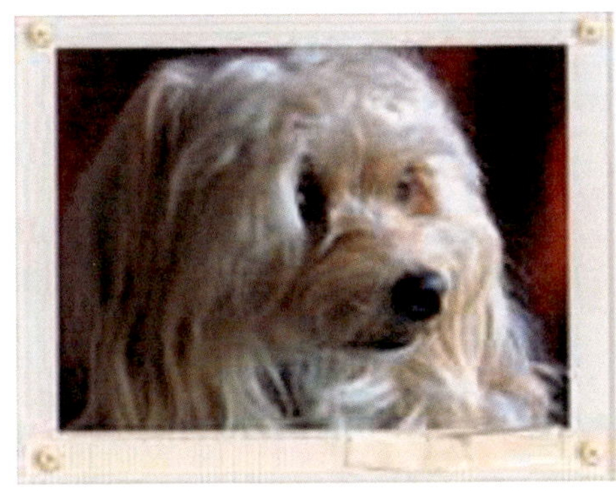

Dear Children,

I am a happy little dog named Chaucer. I live with a grandmother and grandfather in a country house that has many rooms in which to play, and a big yard I n which to have many wonderful adventures.

I often go to school with Grandmother when she reads books to the children. Once when I was very sick (yes, puppies sometimes get sick just like you do) the children had many questions. They asked who my doctor was, how my doctor helped me get better, and many, many other things.

Grandmother asked my doctor if he would help us with this book so you could learn all about what it is like for pets to go to the doctor. I hope you will enjoy CHAUCER GOES TO THE DOCTOR, the 3rd book in my series, "Tails by Chaucer".

Your little buddy,

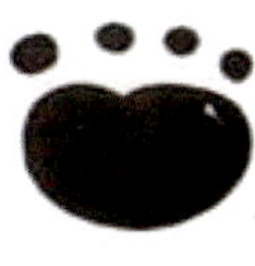

Chaucer

I would also like to give a big "Thank You" and sloppy puppy kisses to Dr. Tom Bruning DVM, and his staff at County Center Animal Hospital.

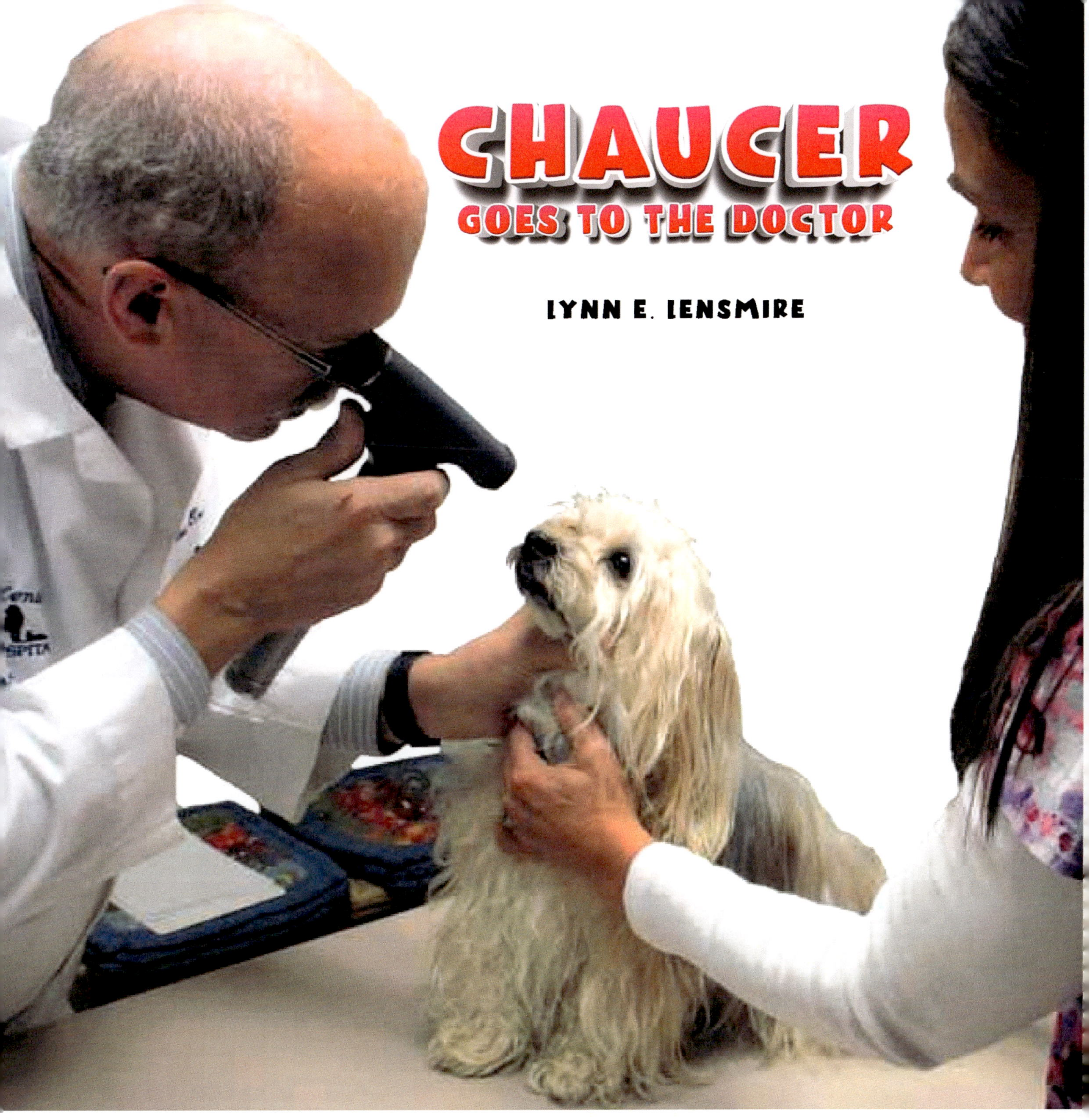
CHAUCER
GOES TO THE DOCTOR
LYNN E. LENSMIRE

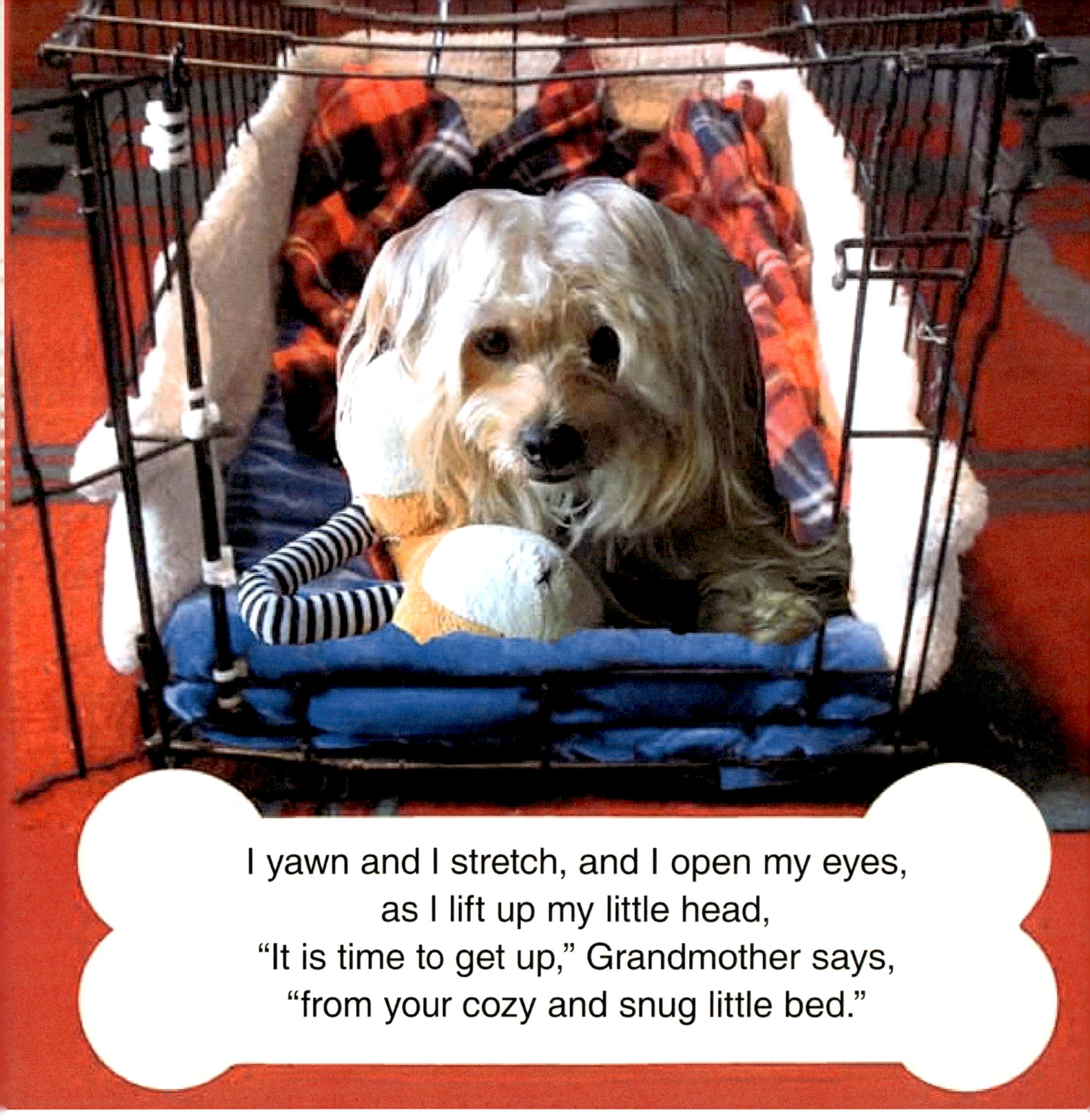

I yawn and I stretch, and I open my eyes,
as I lift up my little head,
"It is time to get up," Grandmother says,
"from your cozy and snug little bed."

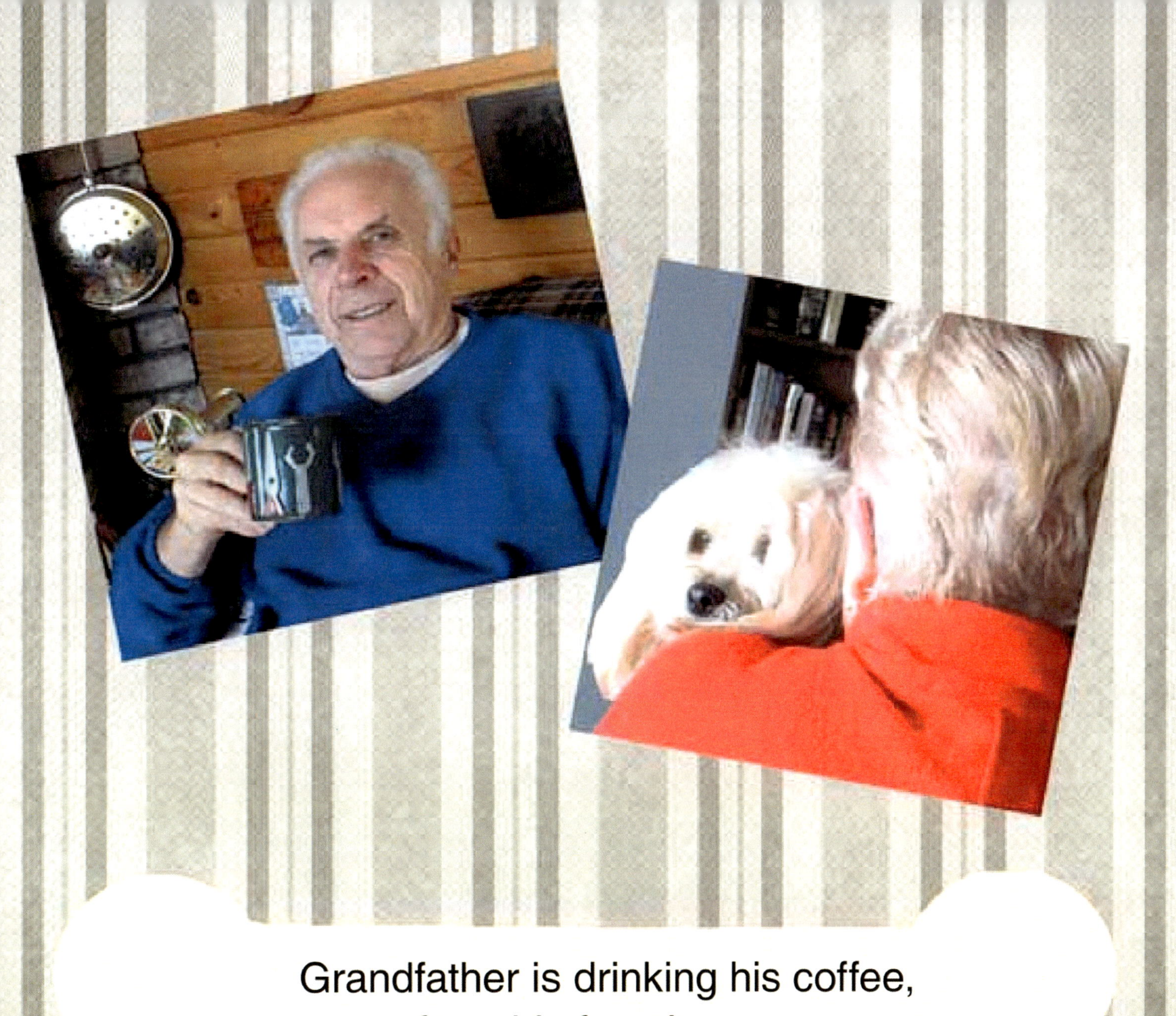

Grandfather is drinking his coffee,
from his favorite mug.
Grandmother swoops me up in her arms,
and gives me a good-morning hug.

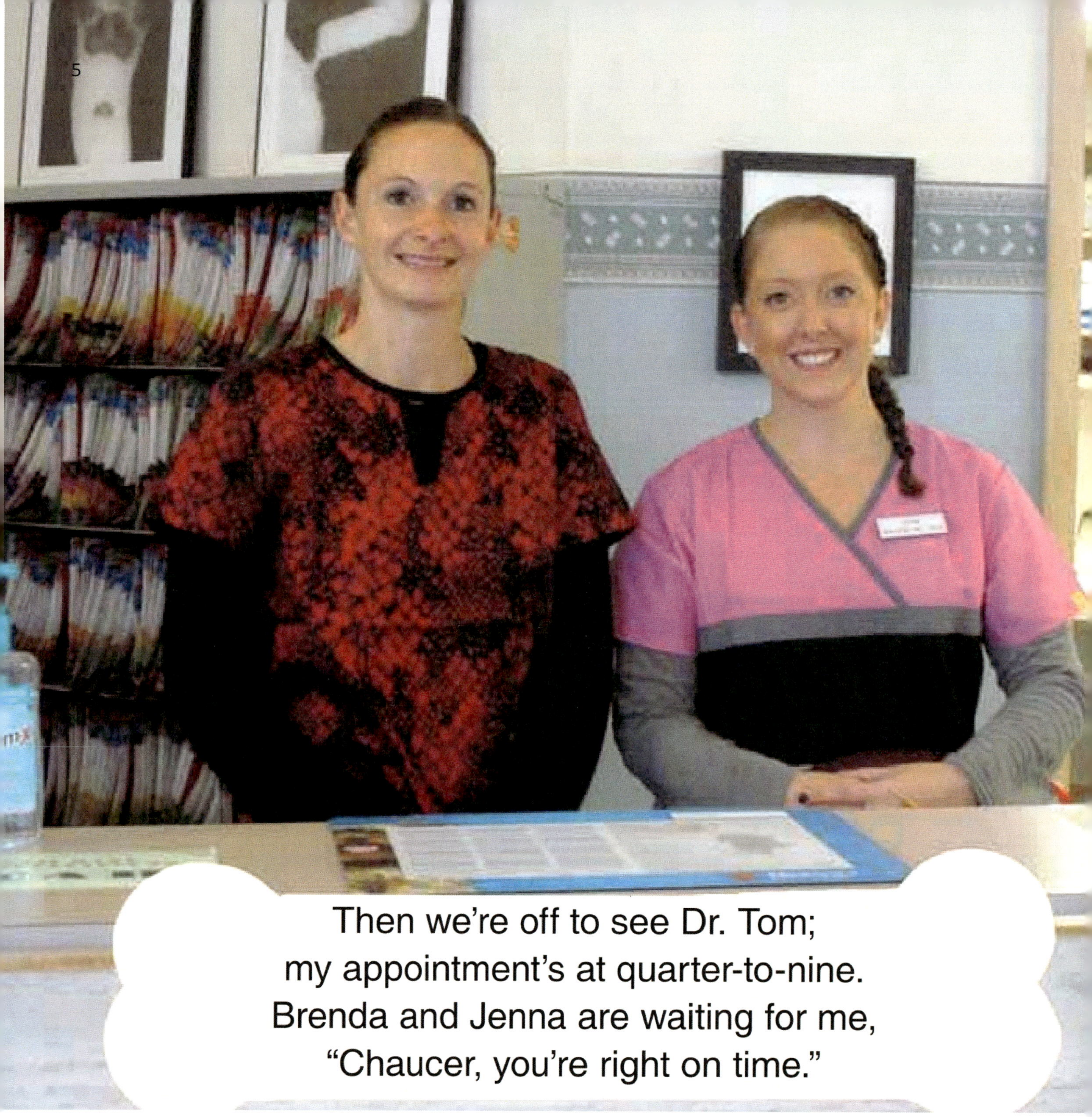

Then we're off to see Dr. Tom;
my appointment's at quarter-to-nine.
Brenda and Jenna are waiting for me,
"Chaucer, you're right on time."

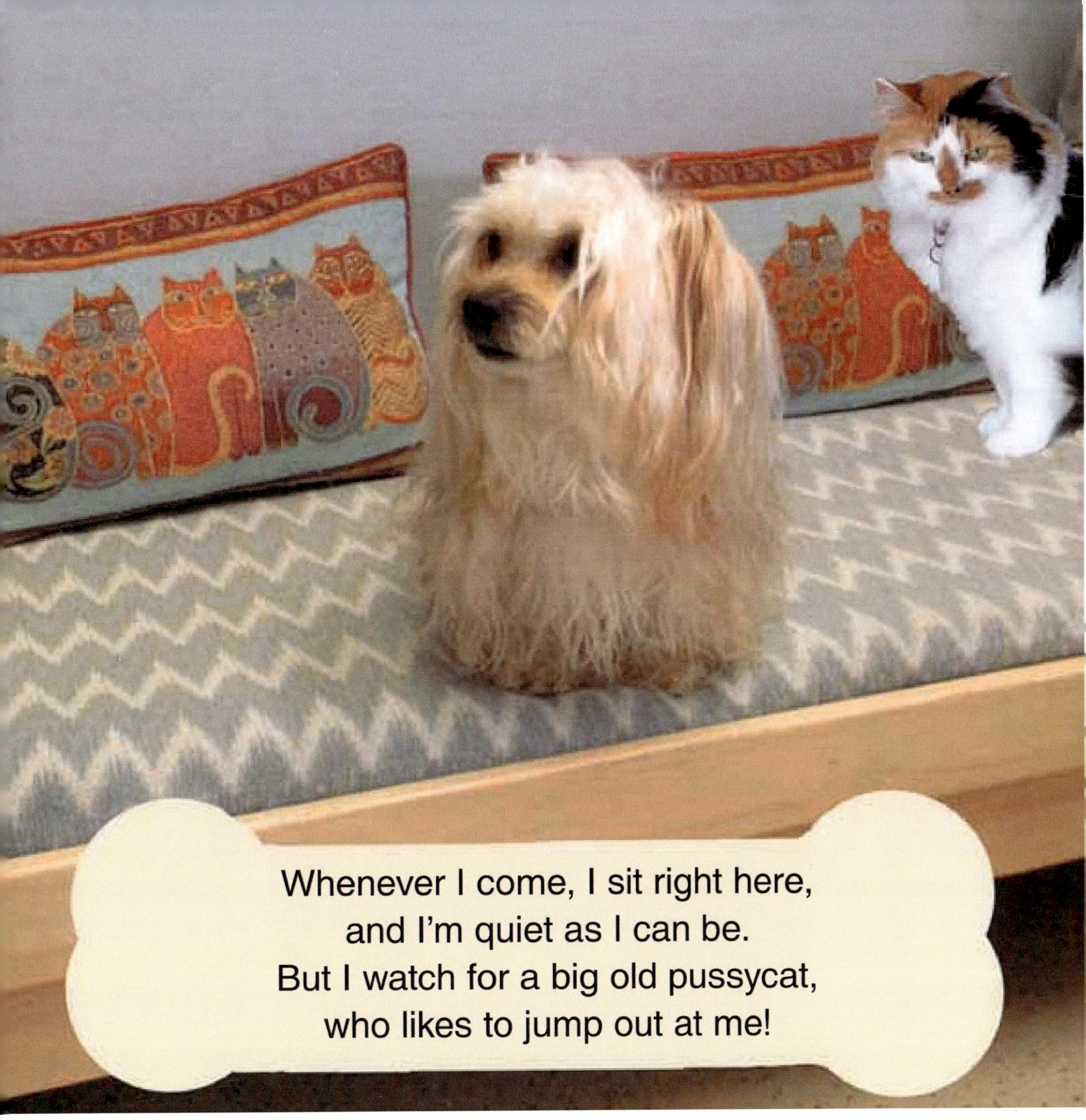
Whenever I come, I sit right here,
and I'm quiet as I can be.
But I watch for a big old pussycat,
who likes to jump out at me!

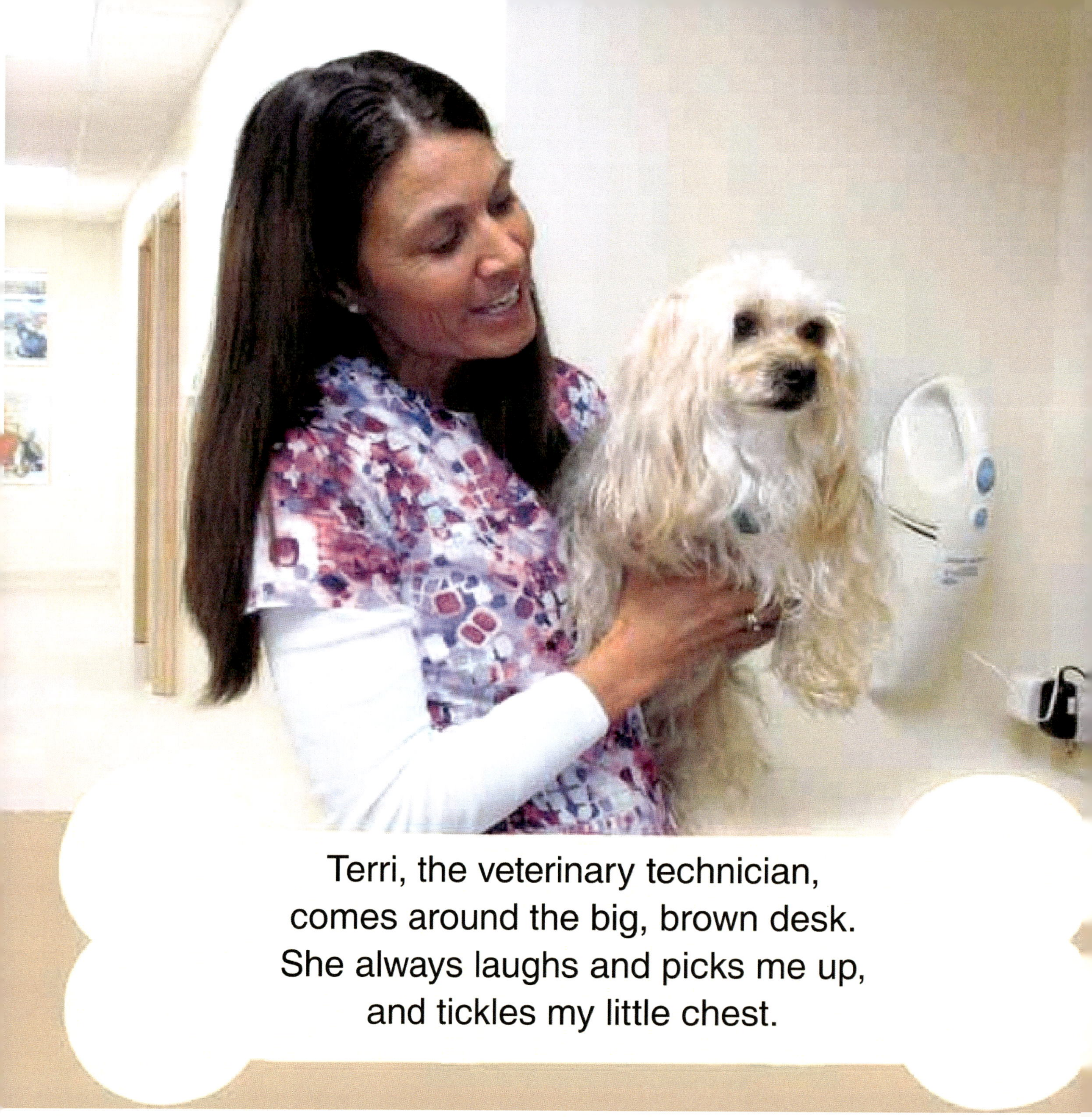

Terri, the veterinary technician,
comes around the big, brown desk.
She always laughs and picks me up,
and tickles my little chest.

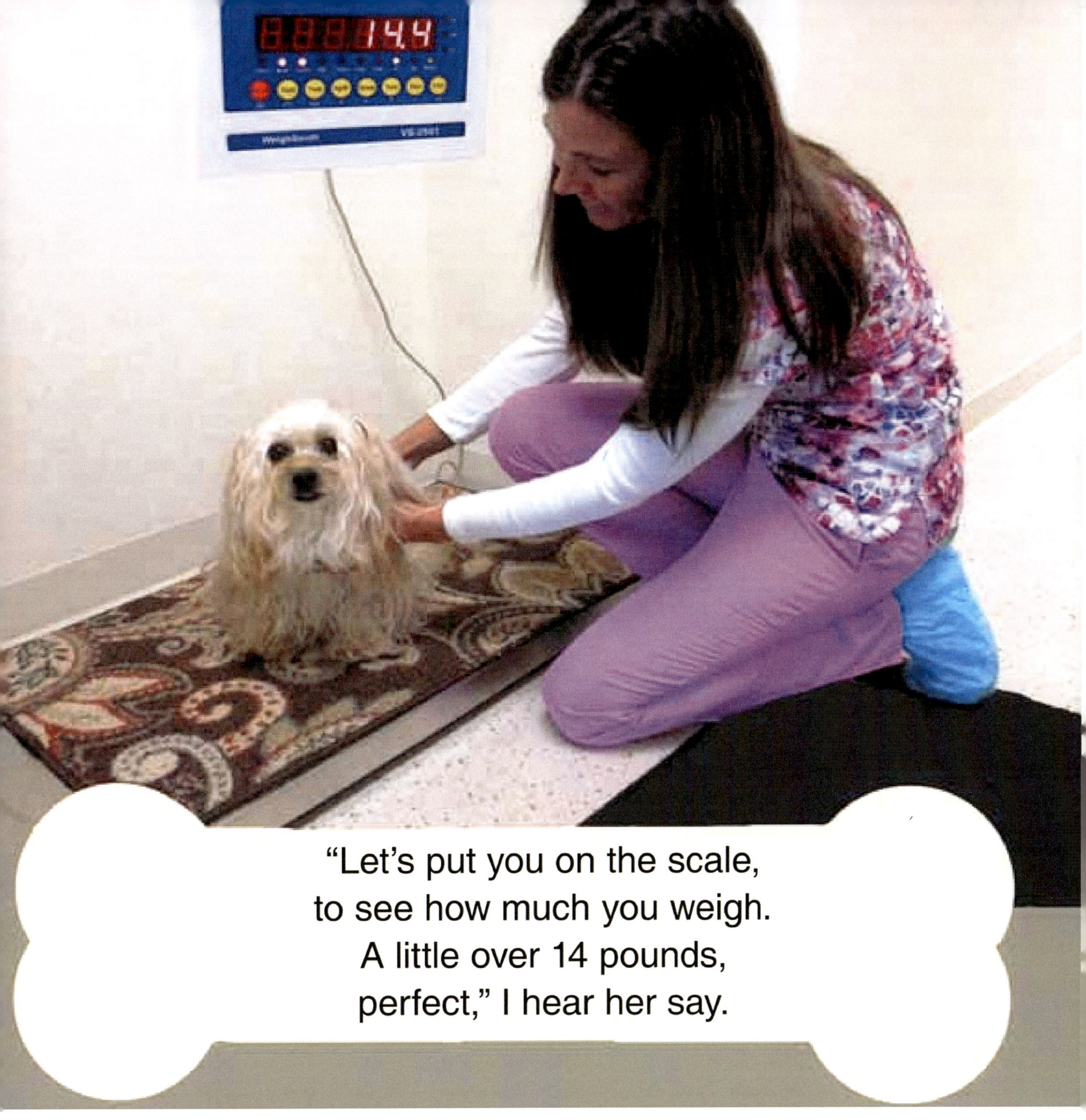

"Let's put you on the scale,
to see how much you weigh.
A little over 14 pounds,
perfect," I hear her say.

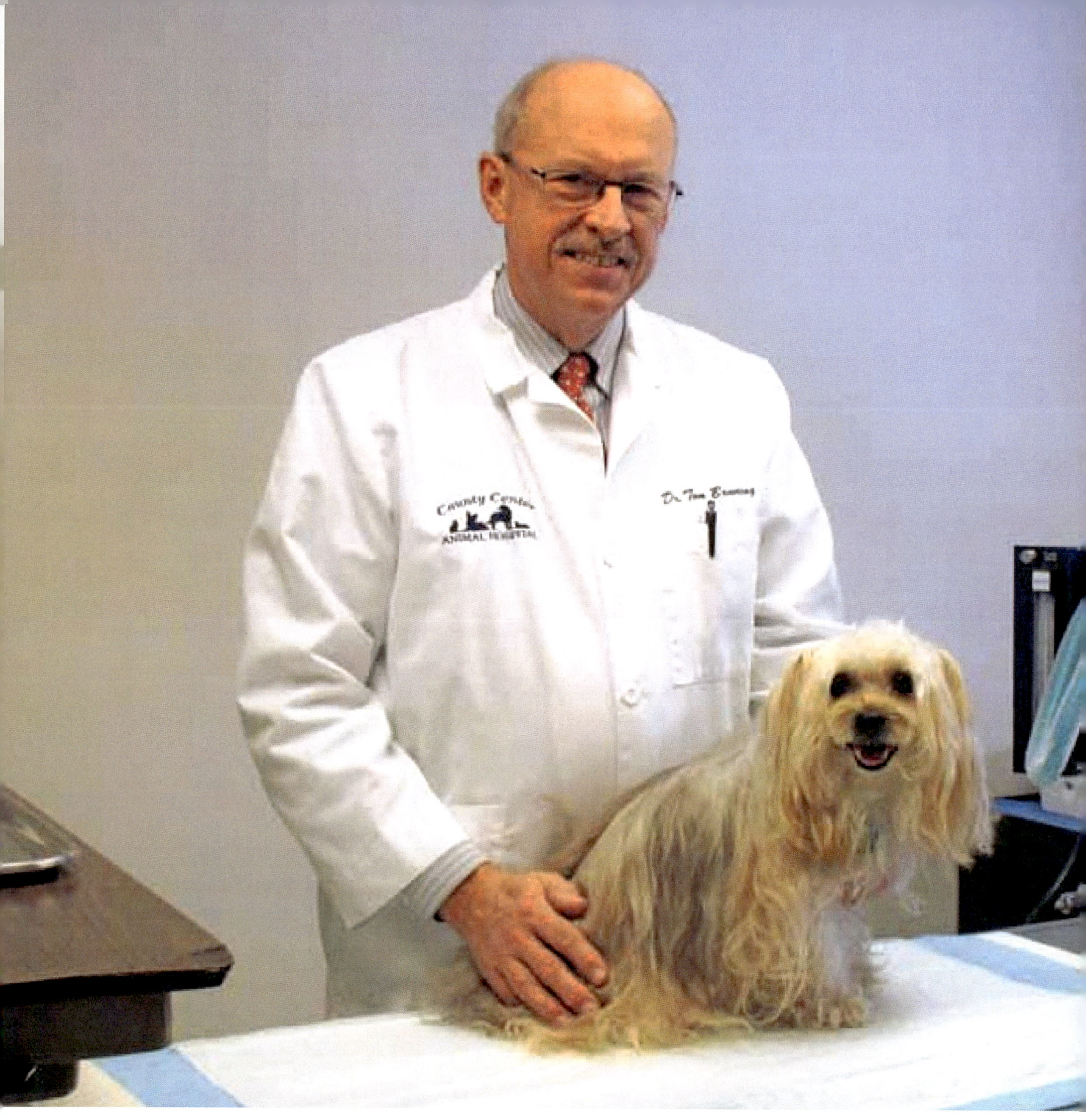
County Center
ANIMAL HOSPITAL

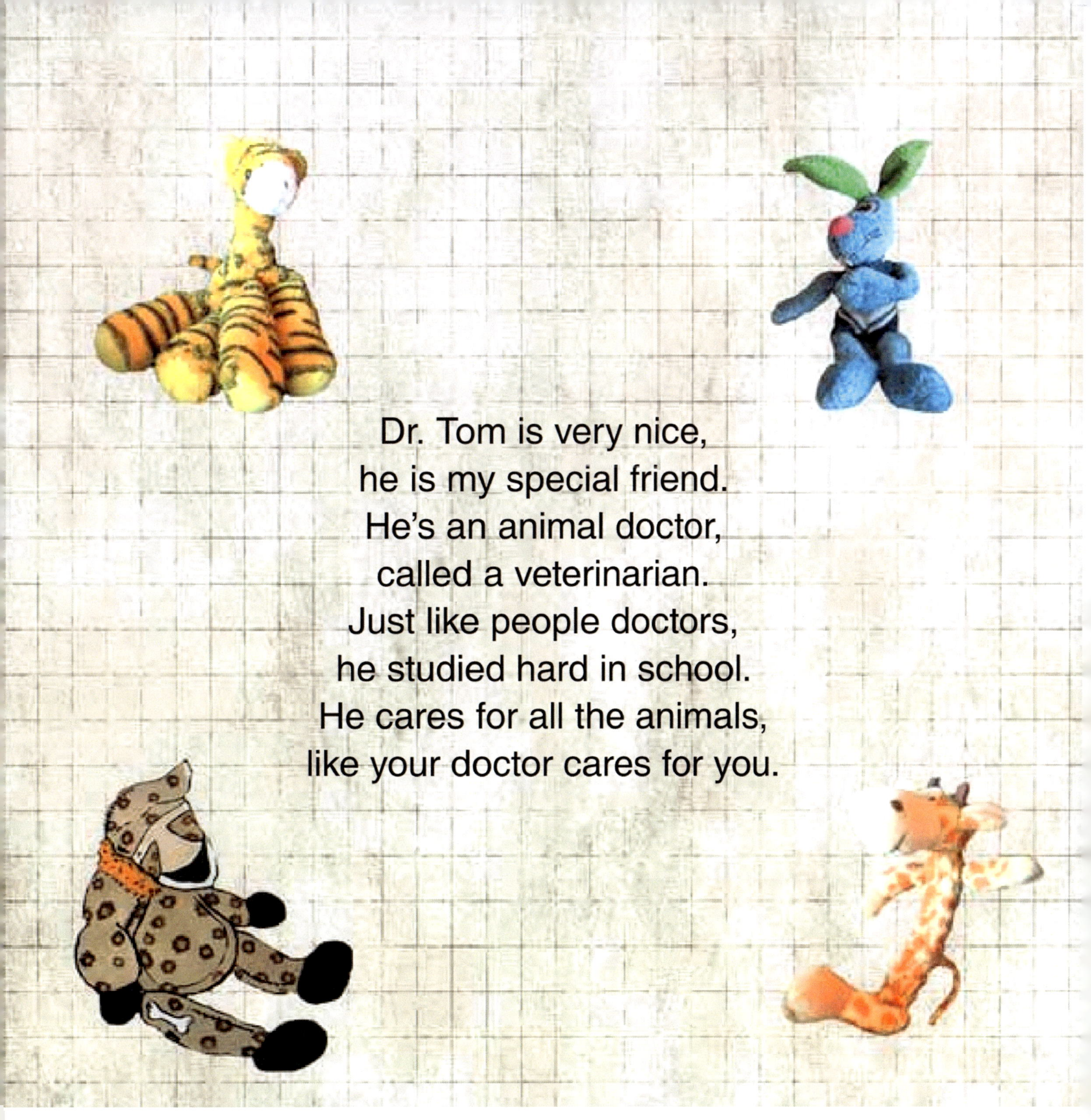

Dr. Tom is very nice,
he is my special friend.
He's an animal doctor,
called a veterinarian.
Just like people doctors,
he studied hard in school.
He cares for all the animals,
like your doctor cares for you.

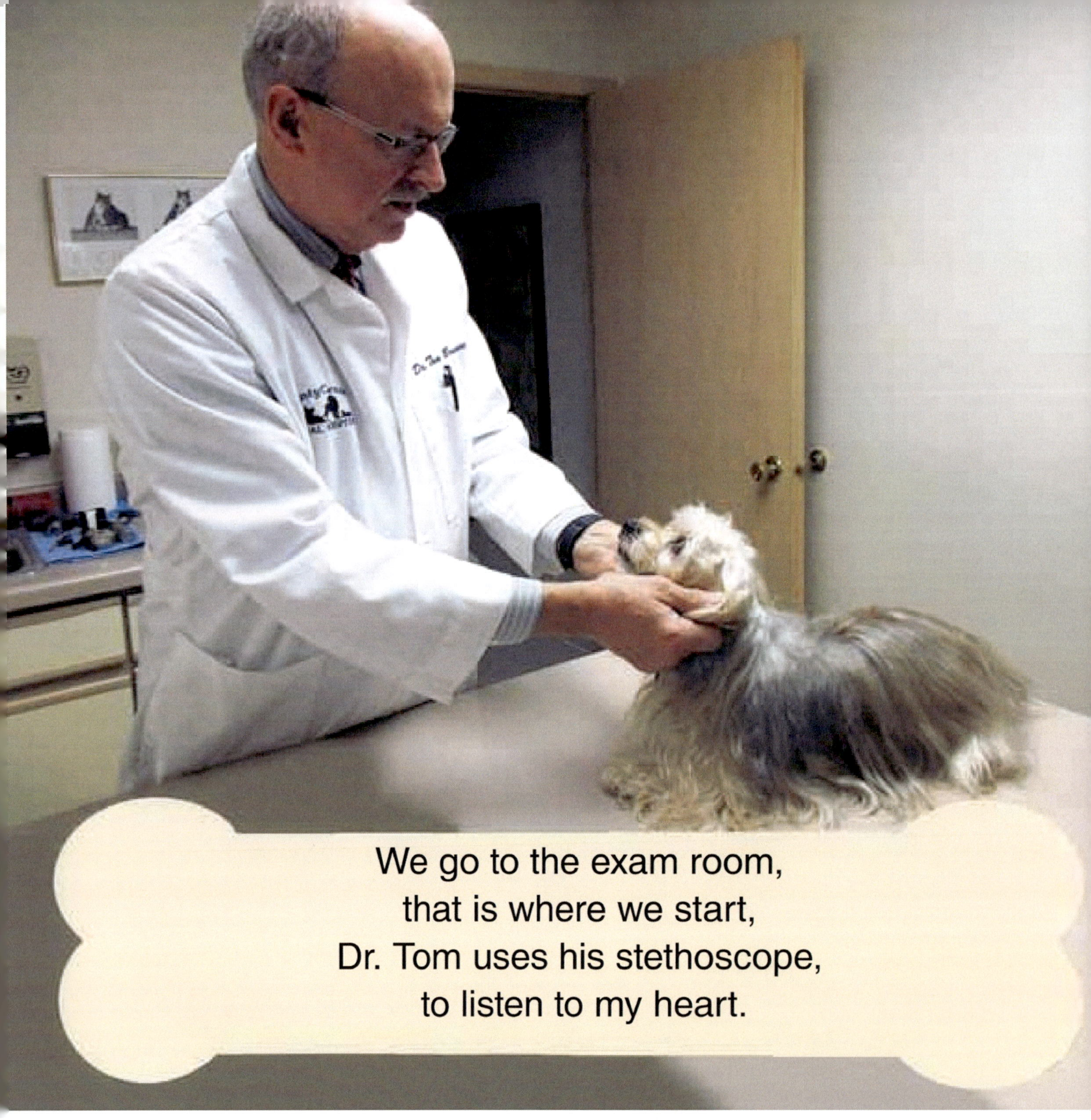
We go to the exam room,
that is where we start,
Dr. Tom uses his stethoscope,
to listen to my heart.

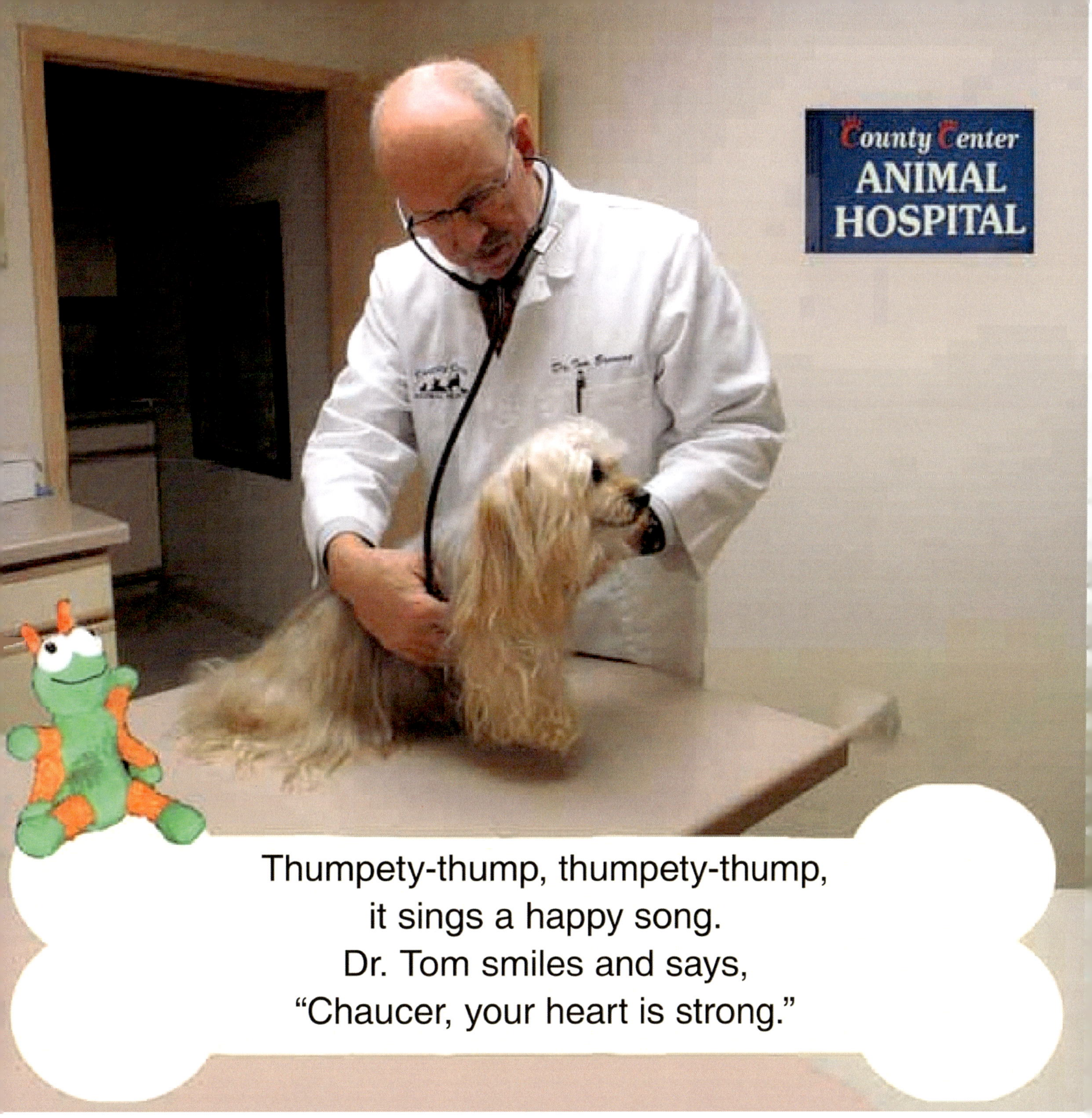

Thumpety-thump, thumpety-thump,
it sings a happy song.
Dr. Tom smiles and says,
“Chaucer, your heart is strong.”

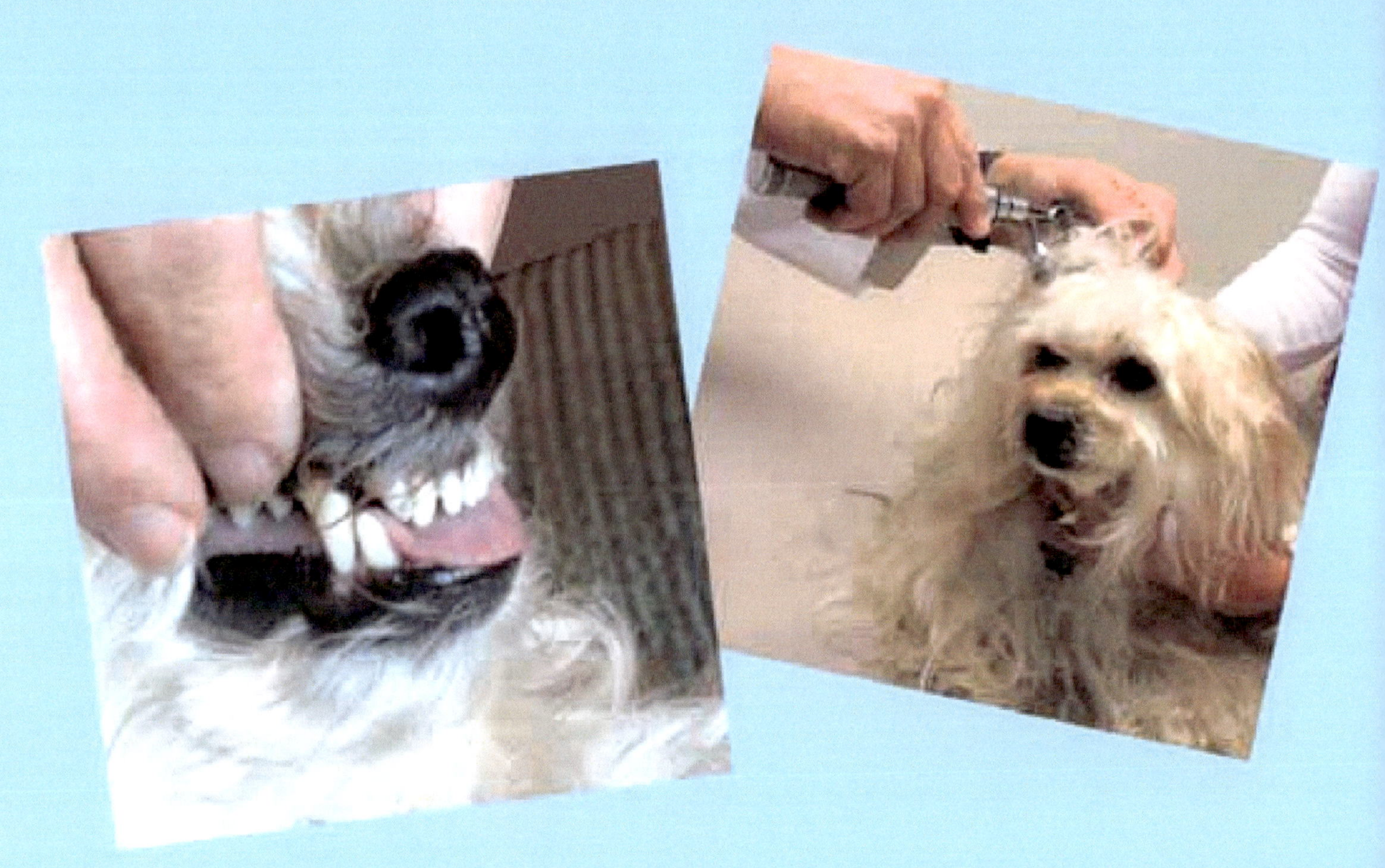

Next I open my mouth up wide,
Dr. Tom likes my pretty white teeth.
He checks my ears…

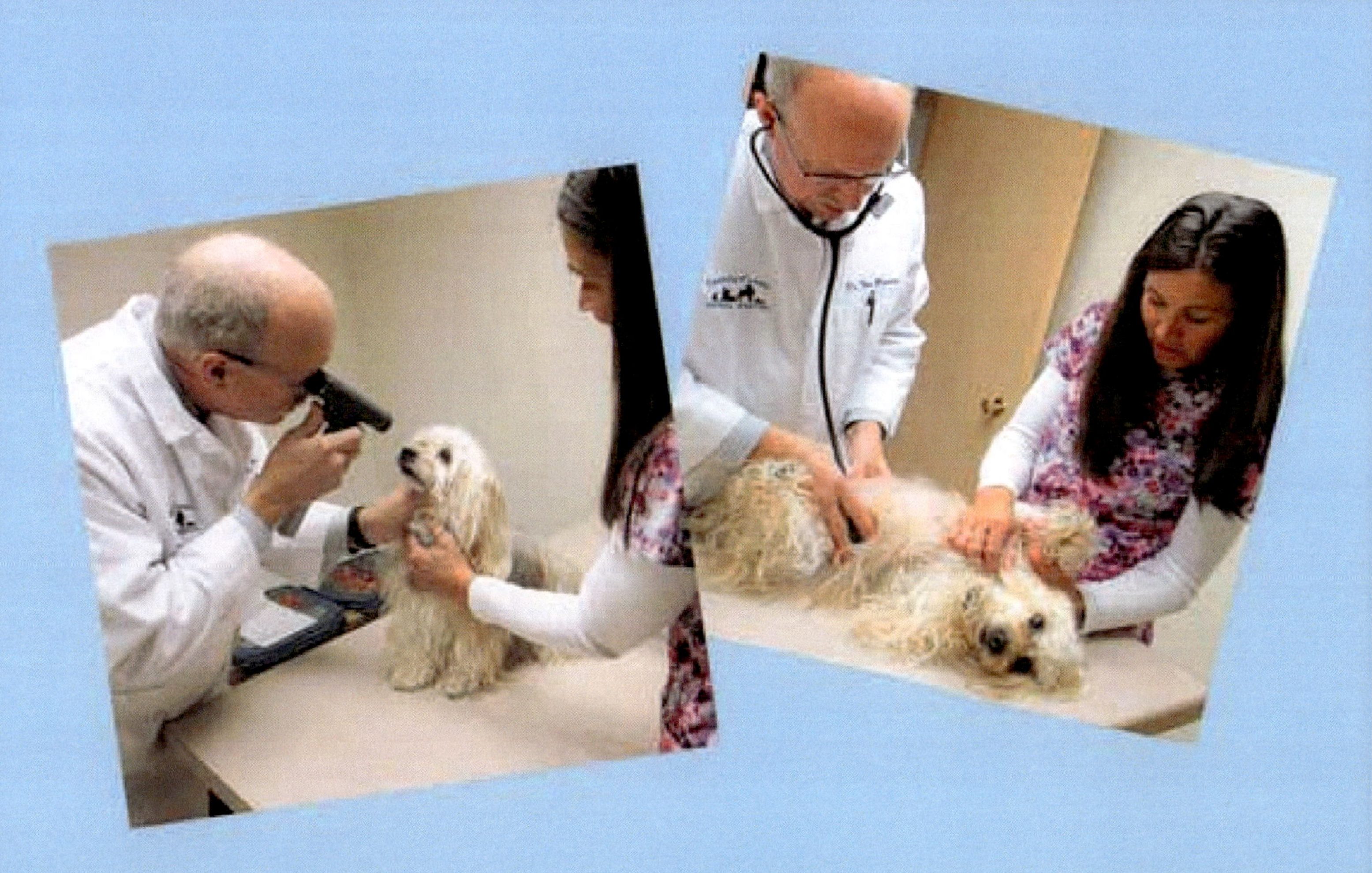

…and then my eyes,
and my tummy underneath.

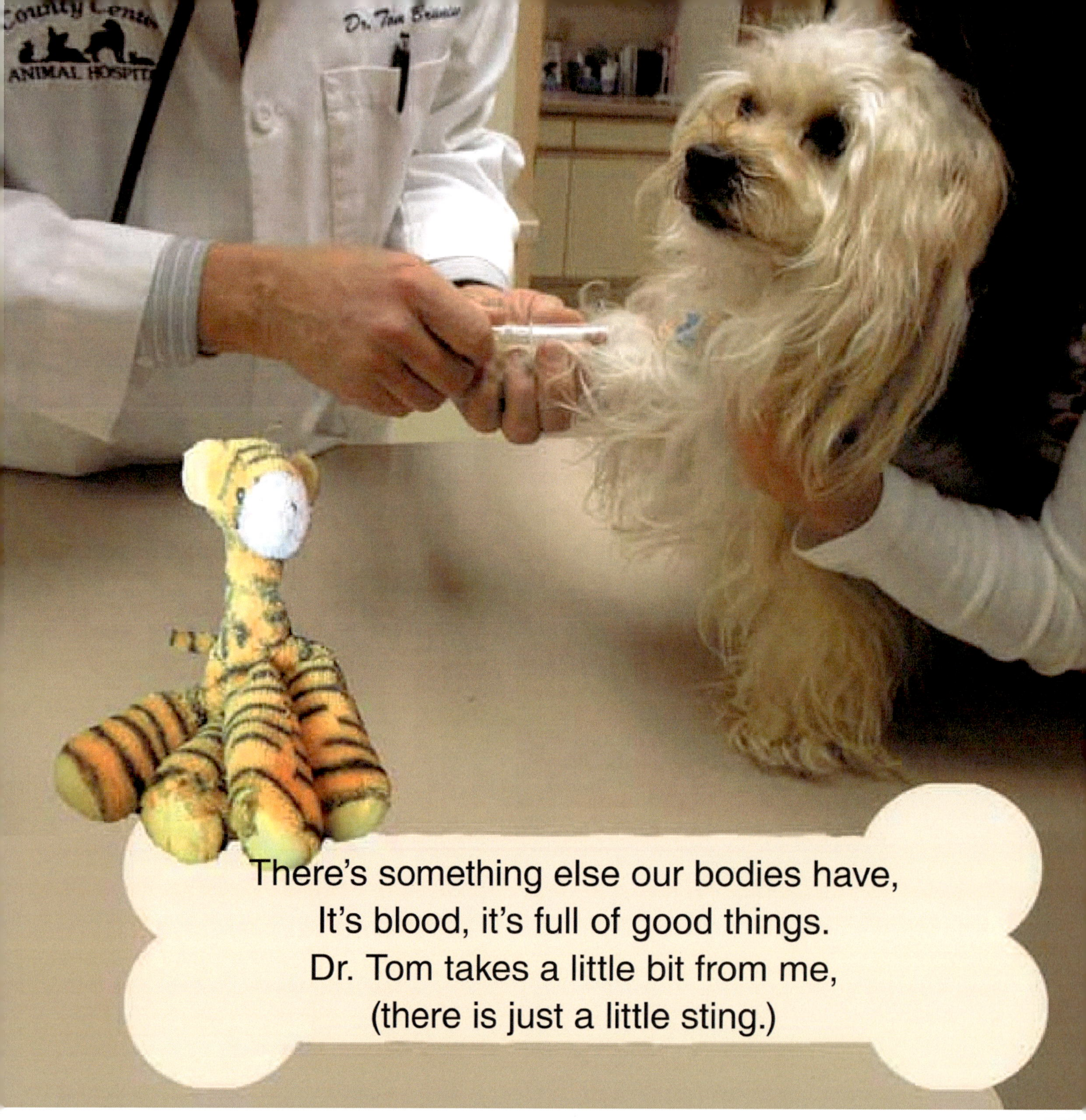
There's something else our bodies have,
It's blood, it's full of good things.
Dr. Tom takes a little bit from me,
(there is just a little sting.)

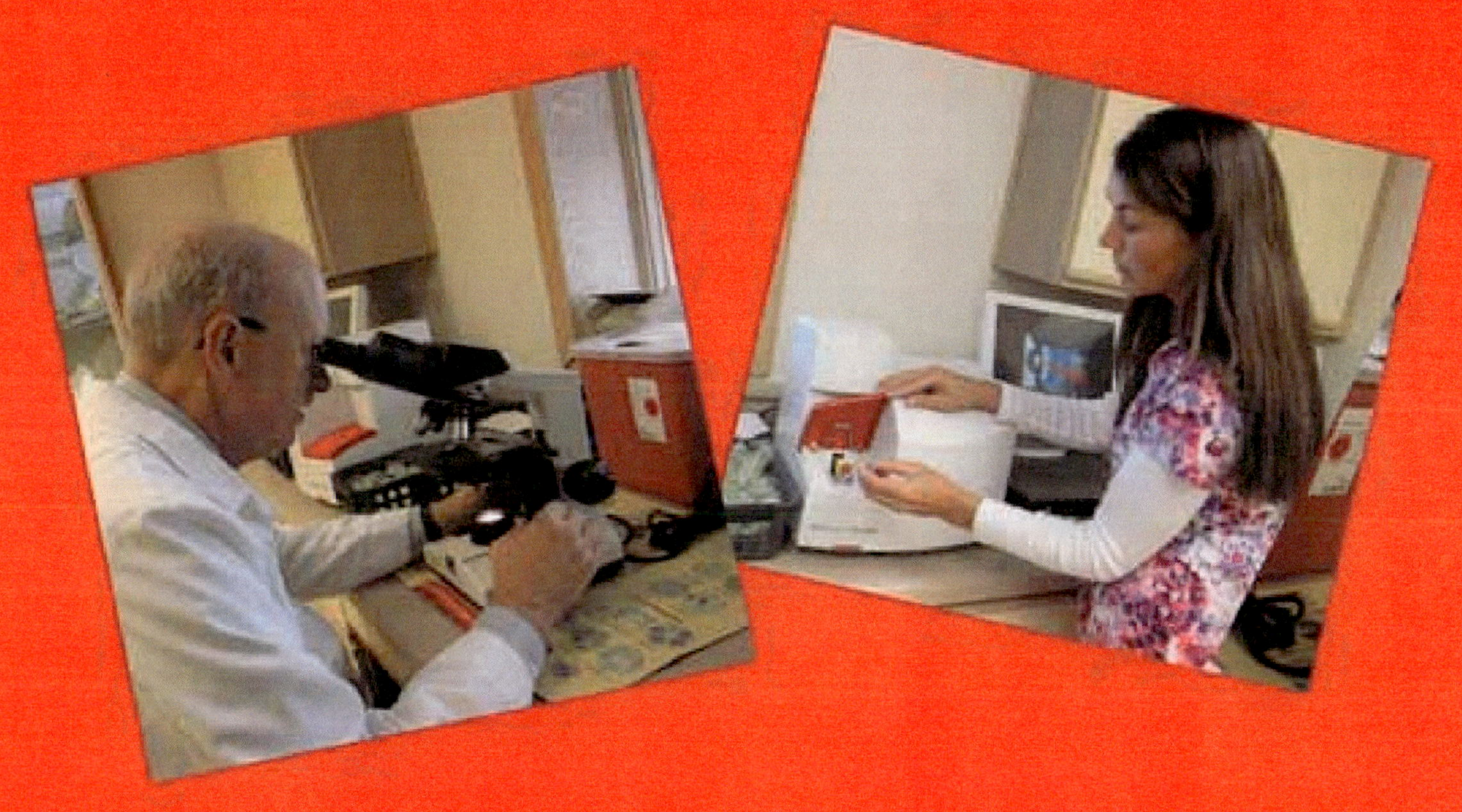

The blood helps doctors figure out,
if there is something wrong.
Then they can take good care of us,
so we grow big and strong.

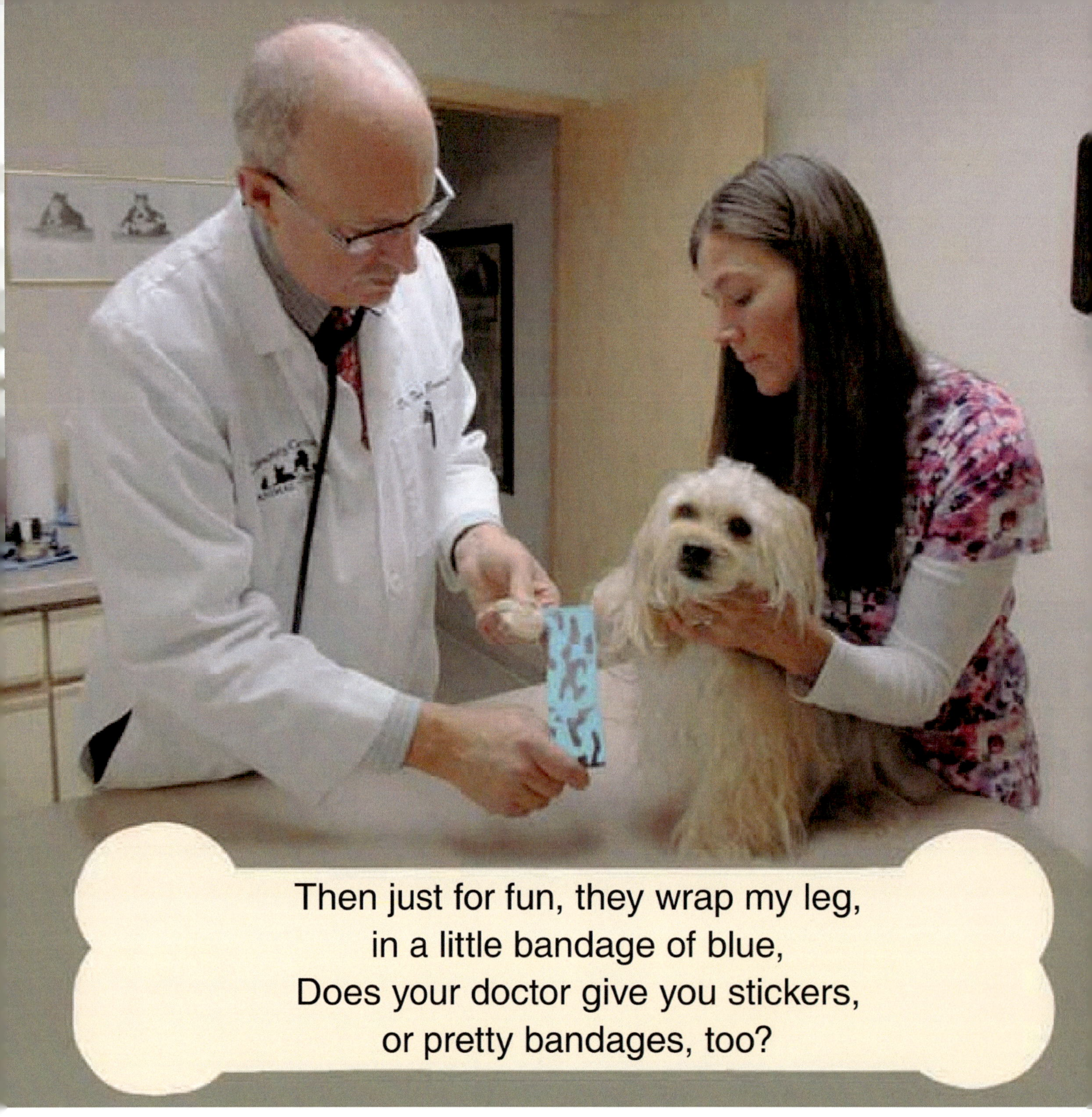
Then just for fun, they wrap my leg,
in a little bandage of blue,
Does your doctor give you stickers,
or pretty bandages, too?

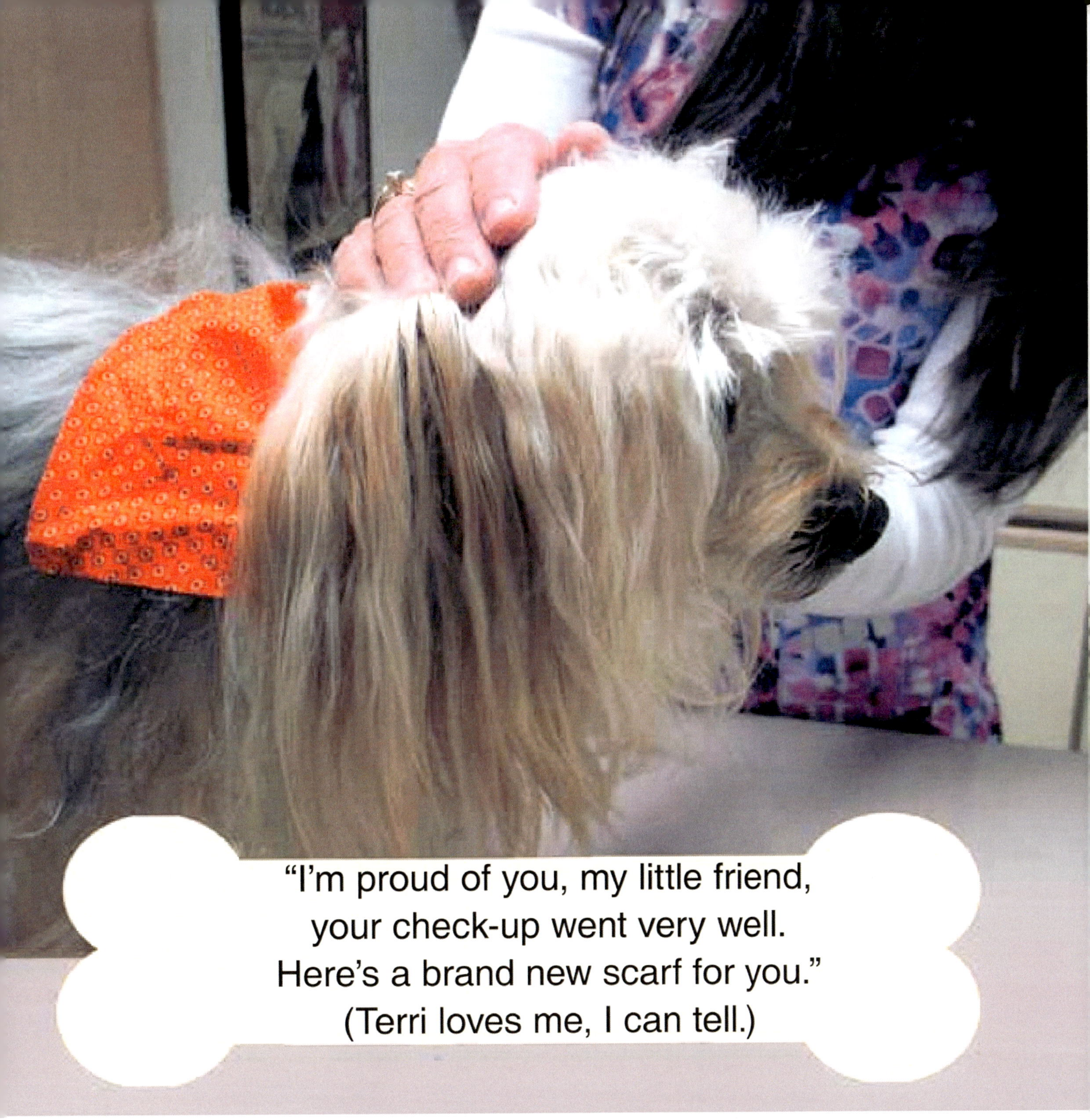

"I'm proud of you, my little friend,
your check-up went very well.
Here's a brand new scarf for you."
(Terri loves me, I can tell.)

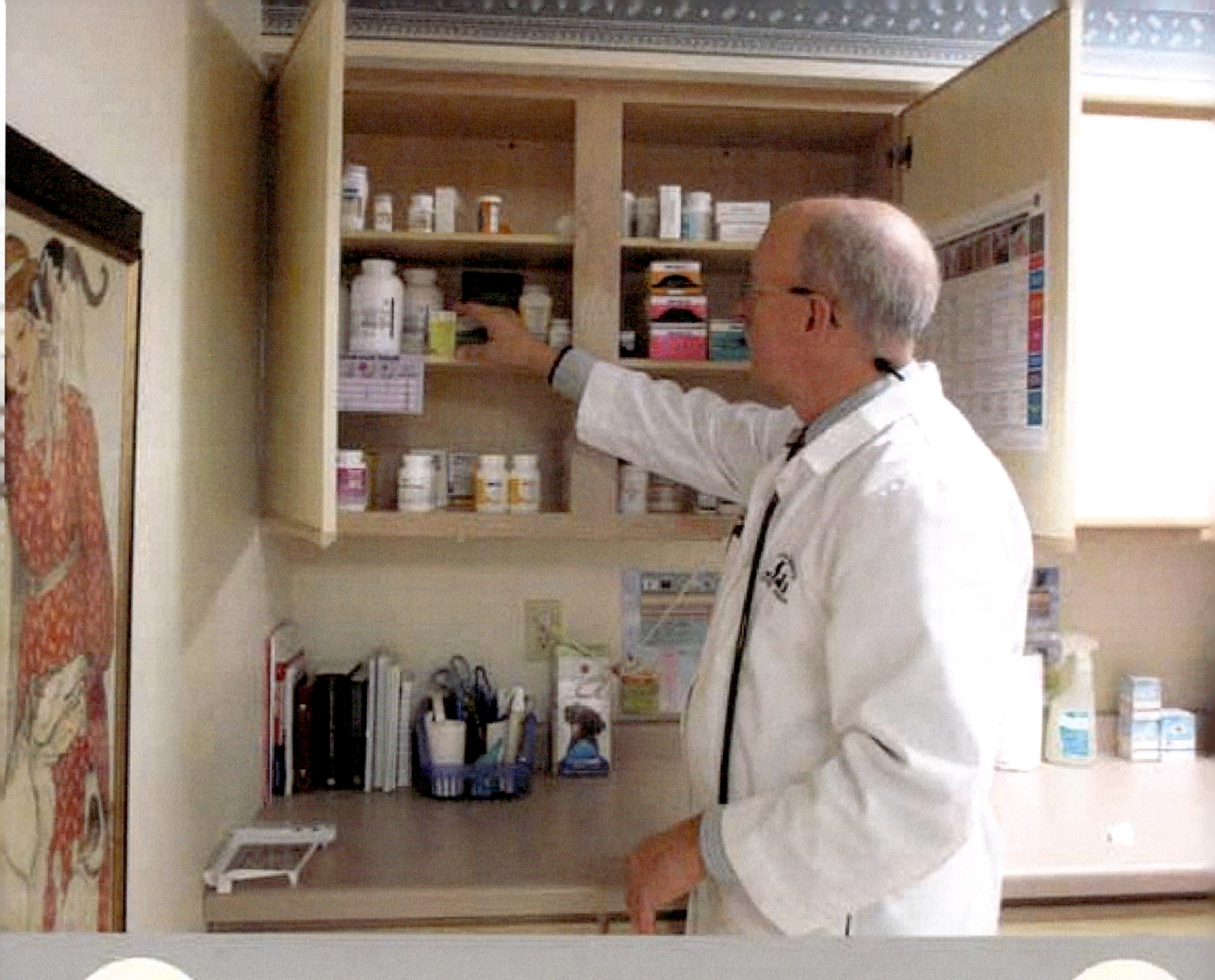

Dr. Tom has time to show us,
other ways he helps us pets.
Like the medicine he gives to us,
that's kept in this cabinet.

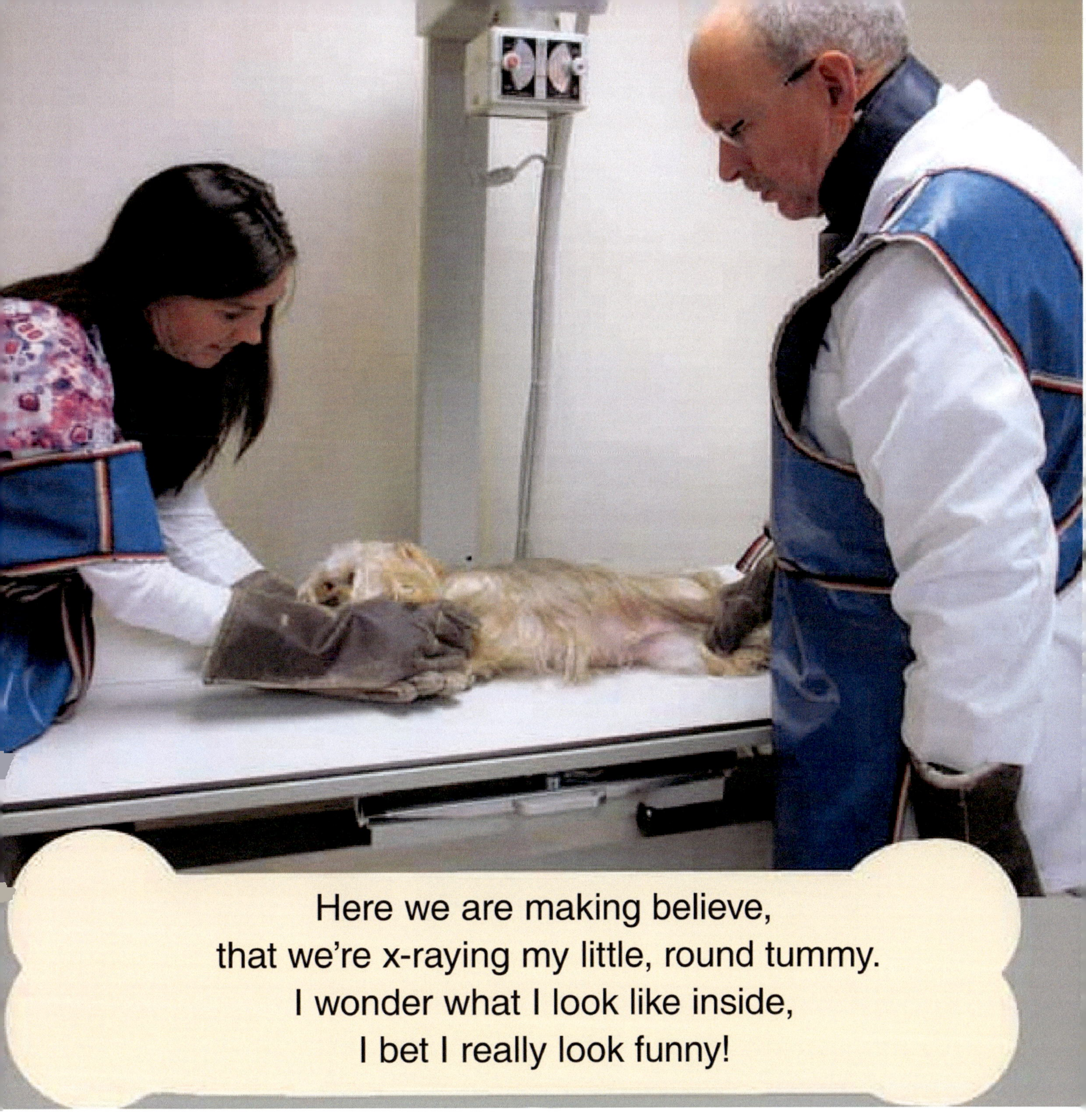

Here we are making believe,
that we're x-raying my little, round tummy.
I wonder what I look like inside,
I bet I really look funny!

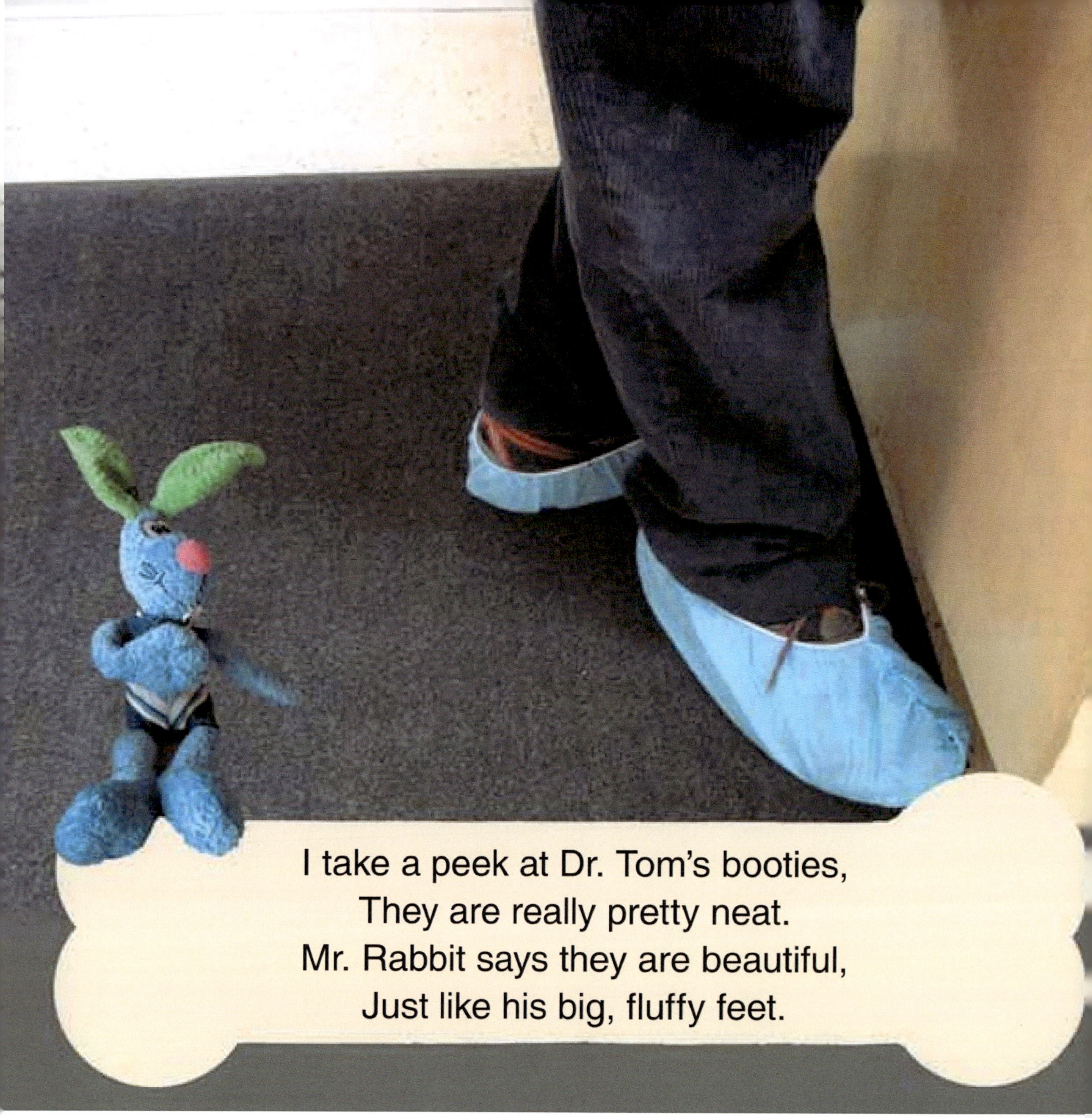

I take a peek at Dr. Tom's booties,
They are really pretty neat.
Mr. Rabbit says they are beautiful,
Just like his big, fluffy feet.

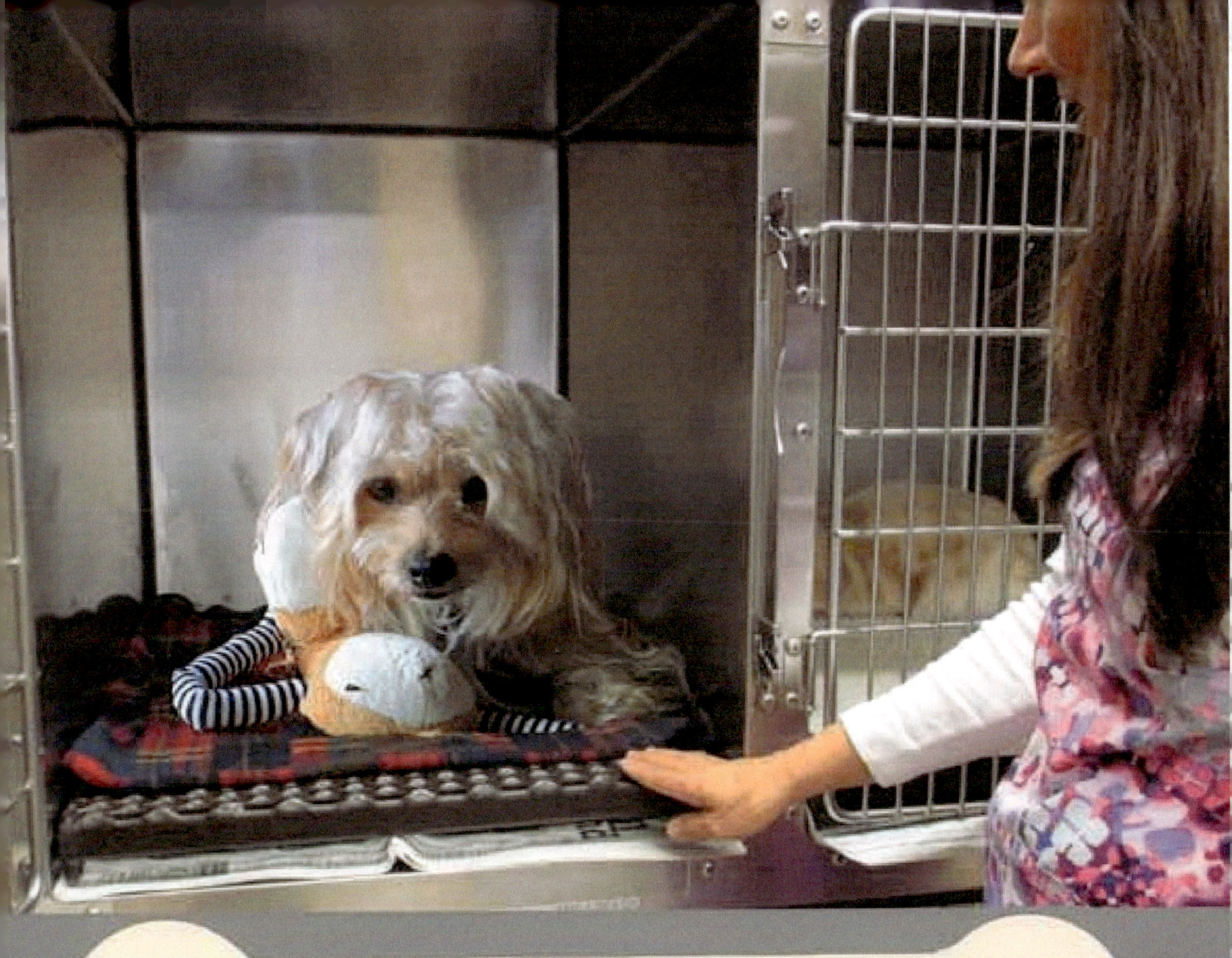

Sometimes pets must stay overnight,
so Dr. Tom can fix what's wrong.
They stay in a warm and cozy bed,
until they can go back home.

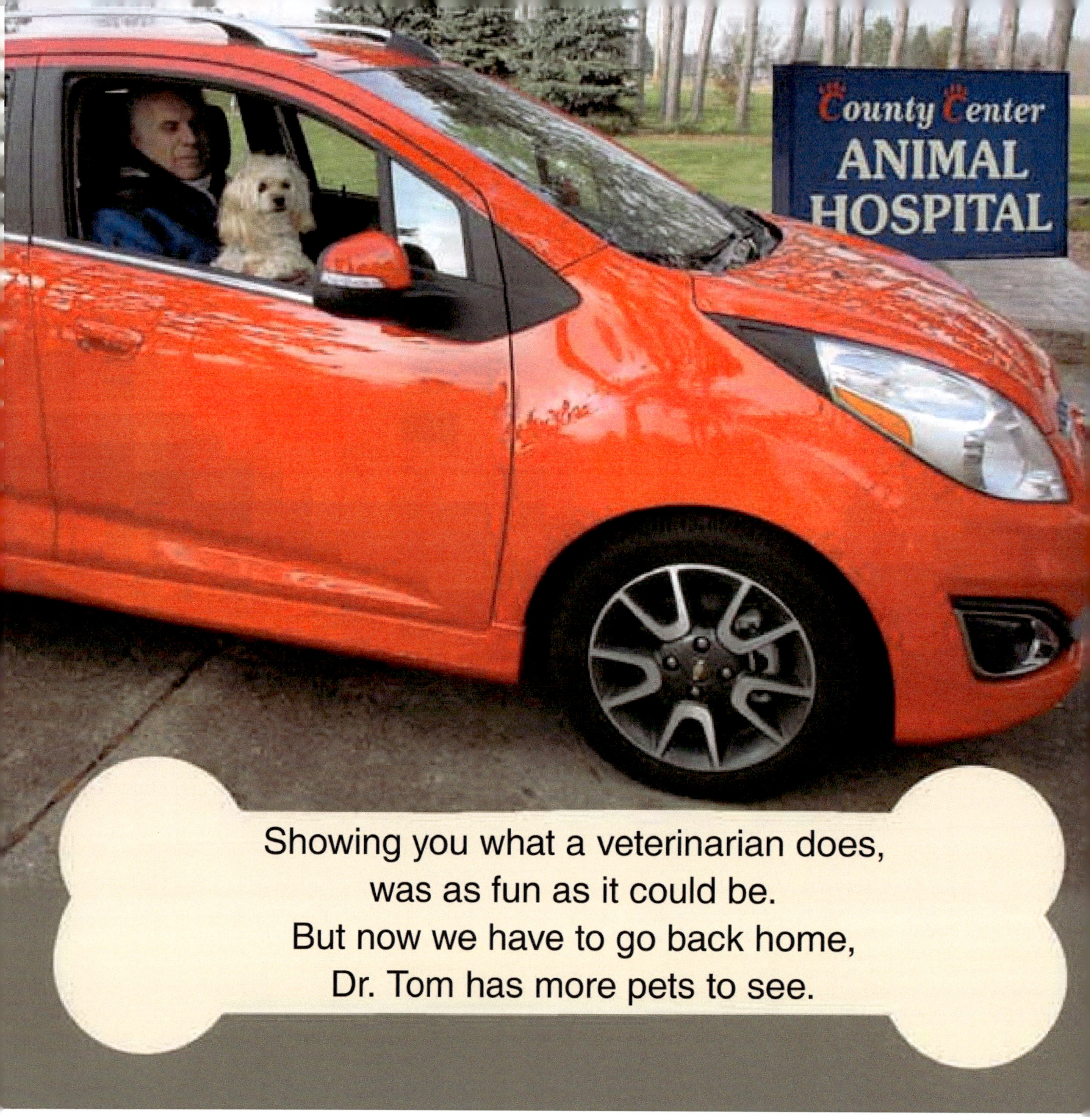

Showing you what a veterinarian does,
was as fun as it could be.
But now we have to go back home,
Dr. Tom has more pets to see.

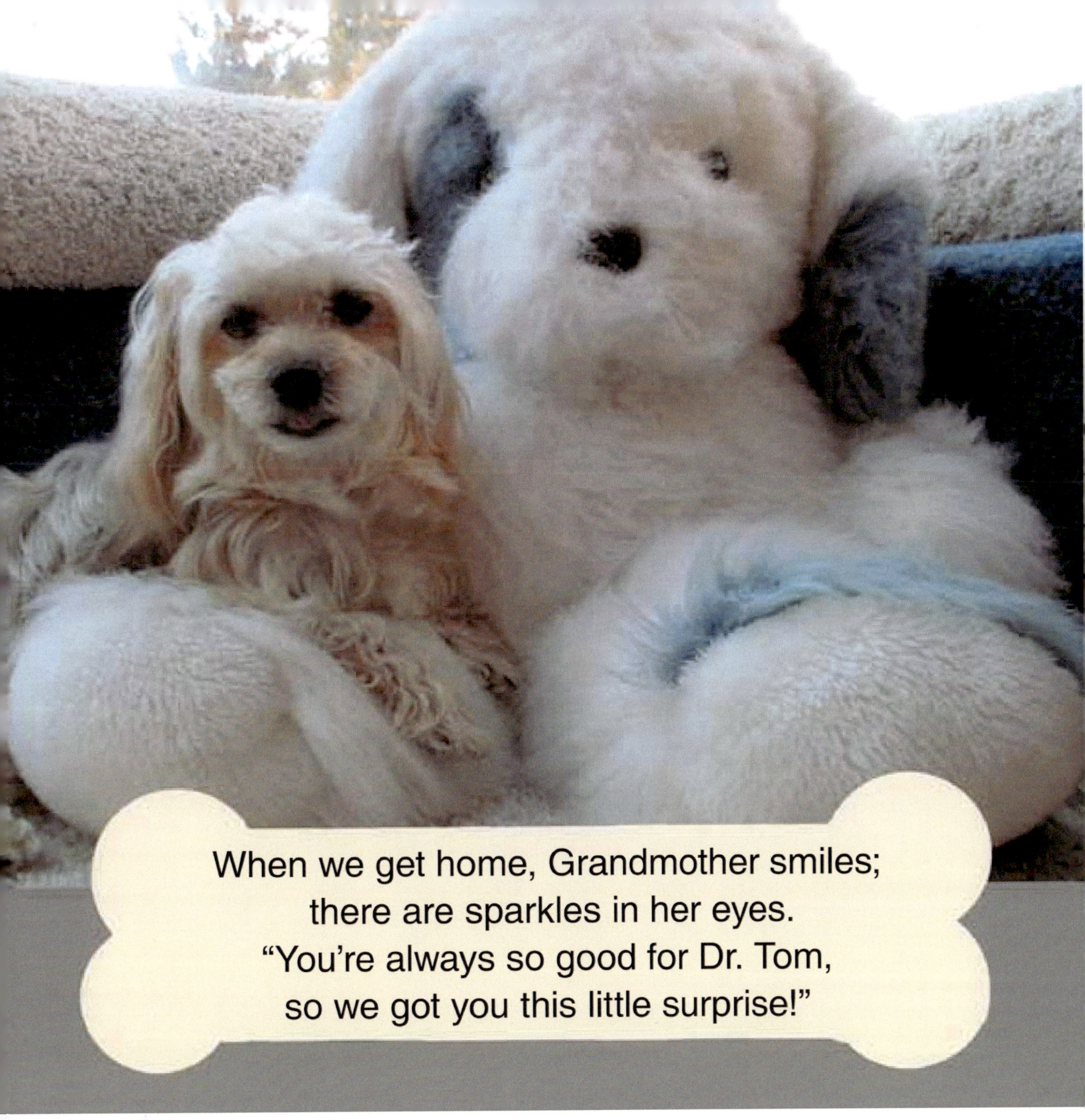

When we get home, Grandmother smiles;
there are sparkles in her eyes.
"You're always so good for Dr. Tom,
so we got you this little surprise!"

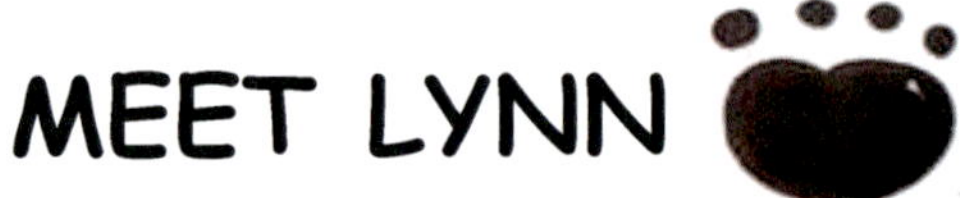

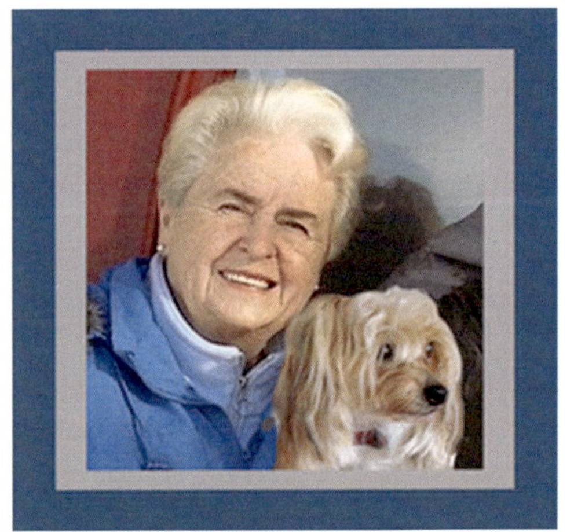

Lynn Lensmire was born in the beautiful rolling hills of central Wisconsin. She grew up on a little farm where she met many creatures large and small, and her imagination created opportunities to know and love them only as a child can. One creature in particular, was the dog, and it is now through the eyes of a little dog named Chaucer that she teaches children important lessons about the world around them.

Lynn's childhood imagination was not lost in the process of growing older, as so often happens. She still believes that sparkling stars can send us special messages, that if you stand quietly under a rainbow when you are sad it will give you a gentle hug, and that snow-covered trees whisper quietly to little animals as they shelter them from the cold.

It is Lynn's prayer that everyone, as they travel life's path, will treasure the joy of imagination, will search for happiness in the simple things in life, and will take time to appreciate the beauty of the world that surrounds us.

www.ingramcontent.com/pod-product-compliance
Ingram Content Group UK Ltd.
Pitfield, Milton Keynes, MK11 3LW, UK
UKRC031356070726
13610UKWH00007BA/11

* 9 7 8 1 9 6 3 3 7 9 5 2 5 *